JavaScript Programming:

A Beginners Guide to the JavaScript Programming Language

Preston Prescott

Contents

Other Books by the Author

SQL for Beginners
http://www.linuxtrainingacademy.com/sql-book

Knowing how to craft SQL queries and navigate your way around a database is an essential skill if are a database administrator, system administrator, or programmer.

SQL for Beginners guides you step-by-step by teaching you how to create databases, populate those databases with data, extract just the data you need, and much more. The book uses plain, clear, and concise language all geared to helped you learn SQL in the easiest manner possible.

Your Free Gift

As a thank you for reading this book, I would like to give you a free copy of "Common Coding Problems Solved Using JavaScript." It's a perfect complement to this book and will help you along your JavaScript journey.

Visit http://www.linuxtrainingacademy.com/javascript-guide/ to download your free gift.

Introduction

JavaScript is the most widely used client-side scripting language that is both really powerful and dynamic. Some of the other popular client-side scripting languages include VBScript and Python. Client-side scripting languages are used to make your websites more interactive, lively, and responsive.

You should never confuse Java with JavaScript. JavaScript is a scripting language, whereas Java is a complex programming language. In fact, the syntax of JavaScript is very much related to that of the C programming language. In 1995, Brenden Eich developed JavaScript. Back then, the language was officially known as ActionScript and appeared in the Netscape browser, which was the popular browser of that time.

You can use JavaScript to help users better interact with Web pages. JavaScript can also be used to control the browser, communicate asynchronously with the server, alter the Web page content dynamically, and to develop games and mobile and desktop applications.

By the end of this book, you will know how to:

- ➢ Configure your environment for JavaScript programming
- ➢ Create variables and arrays to store data
- ➢ Perform mathematical and logical operations
- ➢ Create functions
- ➢ Save and retrieve cookies
- ➢ Deal with Document Object Model (DOM)
- ➢ Make practical use of Object-Oriented Programming

Chapter 1 Setting up Your Environment

Before writing your first JavaScript program, let's see how JavaScript actually runs. This will also help us identify the tools or software applications you need to code in JavaScript.

JavaScript, being a scripting language, cannot run on its own. It actually runs on the Web browser of the visitor, and the browser is responsible for running JavaScript. The happy news is that all modern browsers have JavaScript installed and enabled by default. You do not have to worry whether the visitor of your website uses Google Chrome, Internet Explorer, or any other browser. The browser will take care of running the JavaScript code.

Now it is obvious that you need a browser to see the Web pages you develop. You can use any Web browser like Internet Explorer, Mozilla Firefox, Google Chrome, Apple Safari, or Opera to view a Web page. In addition to that, you will need a text editor to write your JavaScript code. You can use any text editor you want. It can be Microsoft Expression Web, Komodo Edit, Notepad++, or even Notepad. Refer to the Resources section below for links, and download a Web browser and text editor of your choice.

Resources

Web Browsers

1. Internet Explorer
   http://windows.microsoft.com/en-US/internet-explorer/download-ie
2. Mozilla Firefox
   https://www.mozilla.org/en-US/firefox/new/
3. Google Chrome
   http://www.google.com/chrome/
4. Opera
   http://www.opera.com/download

Text Editors

1. Komodo Edit
   http://komodoide.com/komodo-edit/
2. Notepad++
   http://notepad-plus-plus.org

Be ready with any one browser and one text editor. You will be writing your first JavaScript program in the next tutorial.

Chapter 2 An Introduction to HTML

We have already read that JavaScript is mainly used to make websites really interactive, lively, and responsive. So it is apparent that JavaScript needs to be used with Web development languages. HTML is one of the most popular Web development languages around, and JavaScript is used ubiquitously with HTML.

Now we should know where to keep your JavaScript code within an HTML document. You can keep your JavaScript code either internally or externally. In other words, you can keep your JavaScript code directly within your HTML document (internally) or keep your JavaScript code in a separate file and then add a link to that file from your HTML document (externally).

If you do not already know the basic structure of an HTML document, it is

```
<html>
<head>
</head>
<body>
</body>
</html>
```

If you are keeping your JavaScript code internally, then you need to add <script> and </script> tags and place your code between these tags; this way your browser can easily distinguish your JavaScript code from the rest of the HTML or CSS (styling) code in your Web page.

We have also mentioned that there are other client-side scripting languages (such as VBScript). So it is always better to specify the scripting language you want to use. You need to specify the name of the language (in our case, JavaScript) within the <script> tag using the type attribute. So, your <script> tag becomes as follows:

```
<script type="text/javascript">
// Your JavaScript code
</script>
```

You can keep the <script> tag either inside the <head> tag or inside the <body> tag.

Code Sample

Suppose you want to display the current date (in the format dd-mm-yyyy) on your website. Then you need to create an HTML file with the following code:

```
<html>
```

```
<head>
<title>My First Internal JavaScript Code!!!</title>
<script type="text/javascript">
var today = new Date();
var dd = today.getDate();
var mm = today.getMonth()+1;
var yyyy = today.getFullYear();
if(dd<10)
    dd = '0' + dd;
if(mm<10)
    mm = '0' + mm;
today = dd + '-' + mm + '-' + yyyy;
document.write("<b>" + today + "</b>");
</script>
</head>
<body>
</body>
</html>
```

If you open this .html file using your Web browser, you could see the current date in bold letters. If you analyze this HTML file, it is clear that we have added the JavaScript code internally within the <head> section of the HTML document.

As mentioned, you can keep your JavaScript code externally in a separate file, and then add a link to that file from your HTML document. If you want to keep the same JavaScript code in the previous sample externally, then copy the following lines of code into a new file:

```
var today = new Date();
var dd = today.getDate();
var mm = today.getMonth()+ 1;
var yyyy = today.getFullYear();
if(dd<10)
```

9

```
    dd = '0' + dd;
if(mm<10)
    mm = '0' + mm;
today = dd+'-'+mm+'-'+yyyy;
document.write("<b>" + today + "</b>");
```

Save the file as currentdate.js. Now copy the following lines of code into another new file.

```
<html>
<head>
<title>My First Internal JavaScript Code!!!</title>
<script type="text/javascript" src="currentdate.js">
</head>
<body>
</body>
</html>
```

Save this file as displaydate.html. Also make sure that both displaydate.html and currentdate.js are saved in the same folder. If you keep both files in separate folders, then when you set the value of the src attribute of the <script> tag, you should specify the full path to the .js file correctly. If you open the displaydate.html using your Web browser, you will get a Web page that displays the current date.

Now you may be thinking when to go for an internal or external JavaScript code. If your JavaScript code is specific to one or two of your Web pages and you do not have to write too many lines of JavaScript code, then it is better to keep your code internal. On the other hand, if you have too many lines of code that are too common for a number of Web pages, then you should consider keeping your code external.

To further illustrate, say you want to display a table dynamically on your Welcome page. In that case, you can keep the JavaScript code that populates the table within your Welcome page itself. Suppose you want to display the current date in dd-mm-yyy format on all the Web pages of your website, say on 50 Web pages. In such a case, instead of repeating the same code for all 50 pages, you can keep your JavaScript code in a single file and then just add the link to the .js file on all your Web pages.

One main advantage to making your JavaScript code external is that your code becomes easily manageable. Suppose you later decide to display the date in mm/dd/yyyy format. Well, you have to make changes in just that one .js file, and the change will be reflected on all the Web pages that have the link to that file.

So think about your website's requirements before deciding on where to keep your JavaScript code. Reflect on future use in order to make wise decisions.

Chapter 3 Variables and Strings

Every programming language needs to have some option to store data, and that is where variables come into play. JavaScript is no exception. In fact, variables are nothing but data containers. You can use variables to store data or values. You can also use variables in expressions to perform some calculation.

We should assign some unique names to the variables. Though you have the freedom to name variables the way you want, giving descriptive and meaningful names to your variables is a good programming practice. Though variable names can contain letters, digits, dollar signs, and underscores, variable names should not start with a digit. Moreover, you are not supposed to use JavaScript keywords in your variable names. Variable names are case-sensitive, making 'EMPLOYEE' and 'employee' two different variables.

Here are some valid (✓) and invalid (✗) variables:

```
myName ✓
$employees ✓
employee_name ✓
employee5name ✓
_employeename ✓
5employees ✗
let ✗
employee-name ✗
employee#name ✗
employee name ✗
```

Now let's see how to create variables. Before using a variable, you should create (declare) it. You need to use the keyword var to declare a variable, as follows:

```
var totalStudents;
```

You specify the keyword var followed by the variable name and a semicolon. The semicolon tells JavaScript that the current statement is complete (just like using a period after a sentence in English). When you declare a variable, a variable with no value is created. You can assign a value to the variable using the equal sign, as follows:

```
var totalStudents = 50;
```

You also have the freedom to assign a value to the variable as soon as you declare the variable. That is, both the following code snippets are correct.

```
var totalStudents;
totalStudents = 50;
```

OR

```
var totalStudents = 50;
```

You can store not just numbers in a variable. You can also store strings (E.g. "John", "My name is Abel"), Boolean values (true or false), arrays (collection of data), objects (key/value pairs), and even expressions (5+10) in a variable. These different types of data that variables can hold are known as data types. We will see arrays and objects in detail in the succeeding chapters.

When you assign numbers, Booleans, or expressions, you do not have to put the value within double quotes. String values, on the other hand, need to be enclosed in double quotes.

Examples:

```
var myName = "John";
var isSubmitted = true;
var sumVal = 10 + 5;
```

You can easily concatenate string values using + operator. You just need to add a plus sign between the strings to concatenate, as follows:

```
var firstName = "John";
var lastName = "Smith";
var fullName = firstName + " " + lastName;
```

Now the variable fullName will have the value "John Smith." You see that we have added an empty space between the two names.

Many times, you will have to collect input from the user and display it on your Web page after adding some messages. So, how can you get input from the user? It is very easy. You need to use the `prompt()` method to collect input. The `prompt()` method displays a prompt dialog box (with a textbox for the user to enter his/her input) and two buttons: OK and Cancel. After entering an input, the user has to click either OK or Cancel to proceed.

You can directly assign the `prompt()` method to a variable so that the user input will be immediately assigned the variable as soon as the user enters any input.

The syntax of the `prompt()` method is:

```
prompt(message, text)
```

wherein 'message' is the message to be displayed in the dialog box, and `text` is the default text to be displayed in the textbox. The `message` is a required parameter, and `text` is an optional parameter. If you do not specify any value for the `text` parameter, then the textbox will be empty.

Example:

```
var userName = prompt("What is your name?", "Enter here");
```

This code will display a prompt box like this:

You might also have to display your output on the Web page at times. You can use the `document.write()` method to print something on your Web page. Here, `write()` is obviously a method, and for the time being, just understand that `document` is an object with a number of properties and methods that accesses all the elements in the HTML document from JavaScript. We will learn more about the Document Object Model (DOM) in further detail in another chapter.

The syntax of the `document.write()` method is:

```
document.write(exp1, exp2, ….)
```

wherein exp1, exp2, etc., are expressions to print on the Web page. You can have as many expressions as you want.

Example:

```
document.write("My name is John");
var firstName = "Abel";
document.write(firstName);
```

You might have to add comments in your JavaScript code to make it more readable and understandable. Many times, your code will be maintained not by you, but by someone else, and they might not understand the purpose of your lines of code as you do. So, adding comments is really a good programming practice. You can add single-line comments by starting the line of code with // (two forward slashes). If your comment is so big that it spans multiple lines, then start your comment with /* and end it with */. Comments will be ignored by JavaScript.

Example:

```
// Assign the value John to the variable named
firstName
var firstName = "John";
/* This code will display the current date
in the format dd-mm-yyyy
using the JavaScript Date object. */
var today = new Date();
var dd = today.getDate();
var mm = today.getMonth()+ 1;
var yyyy = today.getFullYear();
if(dd<10)
     dd = '0' + dd;
if(mm<10)
    mm = '0' + mm;
today = dd+'-'+mm+'-'+yyyy;
document.write("<b>" + today + "</b>");
```

Exercise

Collect the name and age of the user and display a message in the format "Hi John!!! You are 30 years old." on your Web page. The value John and 30 should be replaced by the values entered by the user. Add comments wisely.

Solution

```
<html>
<head>
<title>Collect Inputs and Print Output!!!</title>
<script type="text/javascript">
//Ask the name
var name = prompt("Please enter your name!!!");
//Ask the age
var age = prompt("Please enter your age!!!");
//Concatenate strings to display the message in the
required format
document.write("Hi " + name + "!!! You are " + age +
" years old.");
</script>
</head>
<body>
</body>
</html>
```

Copy the above lines of code in a new file and save it as an .html file. Open your .html file using your browser and you will get two prompt dialog boxes one by one. Suppose you enter Abel in the first box and 23 in the second box, then your output will look like this:

```
Hi Abel!!! You are 232 years old.
```

Chapter 4 JavaScript Arrays

Many times, you will have to store a collection of items together. We have seen that we can use variables to store data. But what if you want to store the names of 100 employees for later reference? Will it be practical to create variables like employee1, employee2, employee3, etc., up to employee100? Suppose you want to display the names of all employees, then you might have to write the document.write method separately for each employee. In short, it will be not only time-consuming, but also difficult to manage. Here arrays become helpful and handy.

An array is a collection of items. Once you create an array, you can access the items using the index number. The index of the first element in an array is zero. You can create an array mainly in two ways. You can create a variable and assign the values in the array enclosed in square brackets.

Example:

```
var employees = ["John Smith", "Kevin Young", "Hannah
Rivera", "John Joseph"];
```

Here we declared a variable and assigned an array to it with four
names. Now employees[0] will return John Smith and
employees[3] will return John Joseph. You can add more names to
the array like this:

```
employees[4] = "Sarah Rose" ;
employees[5] = "Olivia White"
```

You can create an array using the new keyword as well.

```
var employees = new Array("John Smith", "Kevin
Young", "Hannah Rivera", "John Joseph");
```

OR

```
var employees = new Array();
employees[0] = "John Smith";
employees[1] = "Kevin Young";
employees[2] = "Hannah Rivera";
employees[3] = "John Joseph";
employees[4] = "Sarah Rose" ;
employees[5] = "Olivia White";
```

You can access the individual values in the array using its index
number. You can also use loops to iterate through the values in an
array (See Chapter 7).

Example:

```
var fruits = ["orange", "mango", "banana", "grapes"];
alert(fruits[0]);
```

The array object provides a number of properties and methods that you can use to manipulate your arrays easily and efficiently. You can use the length property to get the number of items in an array. You can use the shift method to remove the first element of an array, the pop method to remove the last element of an array, the reverse method to reverse the elements in an array, the sort method to sort the elements of an array, and so on.

Arrays with named indexes are known as associative arrays, i.e. instead of numbers, associative arrays use strings. In fact, JavaScript does not support arrays with named indexes. However, you can use JavaScript objects to serve the purpose of associative arrays. JavaScript objects are key/value pairs where keys can be numbers or strings. Arrays can be considered a special type of object where the keys are numbers.

When you create a JavaScript object, the key/value pairs need to be enclosed in curly braces, the key and the value should be separated by a semicolon, and the key/value pairs should be separated by a comma.

Examples:

```
var car = {model:"800", type:"Fiat", color:"red"};
```

You can use the for/in loop to access the keys and values in a JavaScript object (See Chapter 7).

Exercise

Create a fruits array with 4 fruit names. Display all the fruits, the first and last fruits in the array, total number of fruits, the fruits array after sorting them, the fruits array after reversing the order, the first fruit after removing the first one, and the last fruit after removing the last one.

Solution

```
<html>
<head>
<title>Array Manipulations</title>
<script type="text/javascript">
var fruits = ["orange", "mango", "banana", "grapes"];
//you can use loop here once you learn it
document.write("The fruits are: " + fruits[0] + ", "
+ fruits[1] + ", " + fruits[2] + ", " + fruits[3] +
"<br />");
document.write(" The first fruit: " + fruits[0] +
"<br />");
document.write(" The first fruit: " +
fruits[fruits.length-1] + "<br />");
document.write(" Total number of fruits: " +
fruits.length + "<br />");
fruits.sort();
document.write("The fruits after sorting: " +
fruits[0] + ", " + fruits[1] + ", " + fruits[2] + ",
" + fruits[3] + "<br />");
fruits.reverse();
document.write("The fruits after reversing: " +
fruits[0] + ", " + fruits[1] + ", " + fruits[2] + ",
" + fruits[3] + "<br />");
fruits.shift();
```

```
document.write("The first fruit after using the shift
method: " + fruits[0] + "<br />");
fruits.pop();
document.write(" The last fruit after using the pop
method: " + fruits[fruits.length-1] + "<br />");
document.write("Now the fruits array contain only " +
fruits[0] + " and " + fruits[1]);
</script>
</head>
<body>
</body>
</html>
```

Copy the above lines of code in a new file and save it as an .html
file. Open your .html file using your browser and you will get an
output like this:

```
The fruits are: orange, mango, banana, grapes
The first fruit: orange
The first fruit: grapes
Total number of fruits: 4
The fruits after sorting: banana, grapes, mango,
orange
The fruits after reversing: orange, mango, grapes,
banana
The first fruit after using the shift method: mango
The last fruit after using the pop method: grapes
Now the fruits array contain only mango and grapes
```

Chapter 5 Math and Numbers

Just having some values in variables will not do any magic. We should be able to perform some operation on the data we have. Operators allow us to perform some operations on operands (the data on which operations happen). Though there are different types of operators, most of the operations are performed on numbers. The operators that perform arithmetic or mathematical calculations on numbers are known as arithmetic operators.

You do not have to worry when you hear "complex" terms like arithmetic operators, operands, and so on. You already know most of these arithmetic operators. Don't you use + to add numbers and - to subtract? The 5 mathematical operators in JavaScript are + (addition), - (subtraction), * (multiplication), / (division), and % (modulus). You know the first four operators, for sure. The modulus operator returns the remainder after division.

Example:

```
var answer1 = 53.5 + 24.5 // answer1 stores 78
var answer2 = 94 - 44.5 // answer2 stores 49.5
var answer3 = 100 * 5 //answer3 stores 500
var answer4 = 180 / 16 // answer4 stores 11.25
var answer5 = 26 % 3 //answer5 stores 2
</script>
</head>
<body>
</body>
</html>
```

Now what do you think is the value of answer6 in the following code?

```
var answer6 = 24 + 8 * 3 - 1;
```

Will it be 95 (24 + 8 =32, then 32*3 = 96 and 96-1 = 95), 40 (3-1=2, then 8*2=16 and 24+16=40), or 47 (8*3=24, then 24-1=23 and 24+23=47)? The answer is 47. Did you guess right? We get this answer because of the operator precedence. Though operators are evaluated from left to right, operator precedence determines the predefined order in which operators are evaluated. As per the operator precedence, multiplication, division, and modulus have the same precedence, and addition and subtraction have the same precedence. Note that multiplication, division, and modulus have more precedence than addition and subtraction. That is why 8*3 is calculated first before + and - operators.

Examples:

```
var answer7 = 24 % 7 * 3 - 1; //answer7 stores 8
var answer8 = 24 - 8 % 3 + 6; //answer8 stores 28
```

Now what if you want to get 95 (24 + 8 ==32, then 32*3 = 96 and 96-1 = 95) as the result of the following expression:

```
var answer6 = 24 + 8 * 3 - 1;
```

You can add parentheses wisely to change the default operator precedence. When you add parentheses, the expression in the parentheses will be evaluated first. If you change the expression as follows, you will get the answer 95.

```
var answer6 = ((24 + 8) * 3) - 1;
```

Here, 24+8 will be calculated first, and the result will be multiplied by 3, and finally, one will be subtracted from the result.

Exercises

1. Create two variables and assign two numbers to them. Do different mathematical operations on those two numbers and display the result in the following format:

First number = 36   Second number = 8
36 + 8 = 44
36 – 8 = 28
36 * 8 = 288
36 / 8 = 4.5
36 % 8 = 4

The numbers 36 and 8 can be replaced by any two numbers.

Solution

```html
<html>
<head>
<title>Let's Do Some Math!!!</title>
<script type="text/javascript">
var num1 = 54;
var num2 = 12;
var sum = num1 + num2;
var difference = num1 - num2;
var product = num1 * num2;
var result = num1/num2;
var remainder = num1 % num2;
document.write("First number = " + num1 + "   Second
number = " + num2 +
          "<br />" + num1 + " + " + num2 + " = "
+ sum +
          "<br />" + num1 + " - " + num2 + " = "
+ difference +
          "<br />" + num1 + " * " + num2 + " = "
+ product +
          "<br />" + num1 + " / " + num2 + " = "
+ result +
          "<br />" + num1 + " % " + num2 + " = "
+ remainder);
</script>
</head>
<body>
</body>
</html>
```

If you run the .html file that contains the above lines of code, you will get an output like this:

```
First number = 54 Second number = 12
54 + 12 = 66
54 - 12 = 42
54 * 12 = 648
54 / 12 = 4.5
54 % 12 = 6
```

2. Accept two numbers from the user. Do not forget to inform the user that the second number should be smaller than the first number. Calculate the quotient and remainder after dividing the first number by the second number. Display the result in the following format:

82/4 ===
The quotient is 20 and the remainder is 2

The numbers should be replaced by the numbers entered by the user.

Solution

```
<html>
<head>
<title>Division!!!</title>
<script type="text/javascript">
var dividend = prompt("Enter your first number");
var divisor = prompt("Enter your second number",
"this number needs to be smaller than the previous
number");
var remainder = dividend%divisor;
var quotient = (dividend-remainder)/divisor;
document.write(dividend + "/" + divisor + " ===" +
"<br />"
```

```
                              + "The quotient is " +
quotient + " and the remainder is " + remainder);
</script>
</head>
<body>
</body>
</html>
```

If you run the .html file that contains the above lines of code, you will get a Web page that asks you to enter two numbers. If you enter 36 in the first box and 9 in the second box, then you will get an output like this:

```
36/9 ===
The quotient is 4 and the remainder is 0
```

Chapter 6 Making Decisions with Booleans and Conditionals

As in real life, programming also has to deal with conditions and decisions. That is, if a particular condition is met, then a specific action must happen; and if that condition is not met, another action must take place. Programming implements conditions with the help of Booleans. A Boolean represents one of two values: true or false. Explaining decision-making in programming terms would be as follows: if a condition is true, then execute some lines of code, and if the condition is false, then execute some other lines of code.

In addition to arithmetic operators, JavaScript also provides a number of comparison operators. We will be using these operators in logical statements to check whether the statement returns true or false. Based on this result, we can make decisions in programming (decide the flow of execution).

Different comparison operators are == (equal to), === (equal value and equal type), != (not equal), !== (not equal value or not equal type), > (greater than), < (less than), >= (greater than or equal to) and <= (less than or equal to).

Examples:

9==5 returns false

8==8 returns true

8===8 returns true

8==="8" returns false as the types are not equal (one is a number and the other is a string)

9!=11 returns true

10!=10 returns false

10!="10" returns false as values are equal (though types are not equal)

5<10 returns true

5>10 returns false

5>=10 returns false

11>=10 returns true

10<=10 returns true

9<=10 returns true

Now let us see how to use these comparison operators to check whether a particular condition is met or not, and to perform different actions based on these conditions. Here is where conditional statements come into the picture. In real life, you may have thought, "If I earn more than $100,000, I will buy a new Porsche. But if I earn only $50,000, then I am going to buy a Toyota. If I earn only $25,000, I will not buy a car and instead ride the bus." In this scenario, you are making different decisions based on different conditions.

Similarly in programming, you might have to perform different actions based on different conditions. In short, conditional statements decide the flow of execution. There are four types of conditional statements in JavaScript:

1. if statement
2. if.....else statement
3. if.....else if.......else statement
4. switch statement

The 'if' statement is used only if you have to check one condition. The syntax of an 'if' statement is:

```
If(condition)
{
   lines of code to be executed if the condition
returns true
}
```

Example:

```
var x = 100;
var y = 100;
```

```
document.write("First number: " + x + "<br />Second
number: " + y)
if(x == y)
{
        document.write("<br />Both the numbers are
same.");
}
```

You can use the 'if....else' statement if you want to check two conditions: execute one set of code if the condition is met, and execute the other set of code if the condition is not met. The syntax of the 'if....else' statement is:

```
if(condition)
{
        lines of code to be executed if the condition
returns true
}
else
{
        lines of code to be executed if the condition
returns false
}
```

Example:

```
var x = prompt("Enter a number");
var y = prompt("Enter another number");
document.write("First number: " + x + "<br />Second
number: " + y)
if(x < y)
{
        document.write("<br />First number is smaller
than the second number.");
}
```

33

```
else
{
        document.write("<br />First number is bigger
than or equal to the second number.");
}
```

You can use the 'if....else if....else' statement if you want to check more than two conditions. You can have as many 'else....if' sections as you want depending on the number of conditions you need to check. For example, if you want to check 5 conditions, you will require one 'if' condition, three 'else....if' conditions, and one 'else' condition, or one 'if' condition and four 'else....if' conditions. It is not necessary to have an 'else' condition. The syntax of 'if...else if....else' statement is:

```
if(condition1)
{
        lines of code to be executed if condition1
returns true
}
else if(condition2)
{
        lines of code to be executed if condition2
returns true
}
else
{
        lines of code to be executed if condition1 and
condition2 return false
}
```

Example:

```
var x = prompt("Enter a number");
```

```
var y = prompt("Enter another number");
document.write("First number: " + x + "<br />Second
number: " + y)
if(x < y)
{
        document.write("<br />First number is smaller
than the second number.");
}
else if(x > y)
{
        document.write("<br />First number is bigger
than the second number.");
}
else
{
        document.write("<br />Both the numbers are
same.");
}
```

If you want to check many conditions, then you can use the switch statement. Unlike the 'if....else if...else' statement, the switch expression is only evaluated once, and lines of code associated with the matching expression are executed. The syntax of the switch statement is:

```
switch(condition)
{
        case 1:
                lines of code to be executed
                break;
        case 2:
                lines of code to be executed
                break;
        case 3:
                lines of code to be executed
```

```
                break;
        default:
                lines of code to be executed
                break;
}
```

Make sure that you do not forget the break statement in each
case. Otherwise, you might not get the correct result.

Example:

```
var today = new Date().getDay();
var day;
switch (today) {
    case 0:
        day = "Sunday";
        break;
    case 1:
        day = "Monday";
        break;
    case 2:
        day = "Tuesday";
        break;
    case 3:
        day = "Wednesday";
        break;
    case 4:
        day = "Thursday";
        break;
    case 5:
        day = "Friday";
        break;
    case 6:
        day = "Saturday";
        break;
}
```

```
document.write("Today is " + day + "!!!");
```

The new Date().getDay() method returns a number for the day of the week, starting from 0 for Sunday, 3 for Wednesday, and 6 for Saturday.

Exercises

1. Collect a number from the user and display whether the number is odd or even.

Solution

```
var num = prompt("Enter a number");
if(num%2==0)
    document.write("The number " + num + " is even.");
else
    document.write("The number " + num + " is odd.");
```

2. Display the message "Good Morning!!! Now the time is HH:MM AM." in the morning. Good Morning should be changed to Good Afternoon in the afternoon and Good Evening in the evening. HH and MM should be replaced by hours and minutes respectively. AM and PM values should be displayed correctly.

Tip: You can get the hours and minutes values using the getHours() (in a 24-hour format) and the getMinutes() method of the Date object. If the hours value is less than 12, display Good Morning; if the hours value is between 12 and 16 (4 PM) display Good Evening.

Solution

```
<!DOCTYPE html>
<html>
<head>
<title>Current Time</title>
<script type="text/javascript">
var today = new Date();
var hours = today.getHours();
var minutes = today.getMinutes();

//get the message correctly
var wish;
if(hours<12)
        wish = "Good Morning!!!";
else if(hours<16)
        wish = "Good Afternoon!!!";
else
        wish = "Good Evening!!!";

/*make the hours and minutes in HH and MM format
(adding 0 at the beginning)
 if the value is less than 10*/
if(hours < 10)
        hours = "0" + hours;
if(minutes < 10)
        minutes = "0" + minutes;

//add the value AM or PM correctly
var period;
if(hours <12)
        period = "AM"
else
        period = "PM";

//displaying the message in the required format
```

```
document.write(wish + " Now the time is " + hours +
":" + minutes + " " + period + ".");
</script>
</head>
<body>
</body>
</html>
```

3. Ask for the favorite color of the user and display different messages. Add unique messages for red, green, white, and blue, and a generic message for all remaining colors using the switch loop.

Solution

```
<!DOCTYPE html>
<html>
<head>
<title>Favorite Color</title>
<script type="text/javascript">
var favColor = prompt("Enter your favorite color");
//we convert the input to lower case for case
insensitive comparison
var expression = favColor.toLowerCase();
var message;
switch (expression)
{
case "red":
        message = "Red!!! Mine is also red.";
        break;
case "blue":
        message = "Blue!!!Great color sense!!!";
        break;
case "white":
        message = "White!!! You are too simple.";
```

```
        break;
case "green":
        message = "Green!!! You love to be loved";
        break;
default:
        message = favColor + "!!! Not a bad choice.";
        break;
}
document.write(message);
</script>
</head>
<body>
</body>
</html>
```

Chapter 7 Loops

You may sometimes have to execute a set of instructions repeatedly. For example, you want to display numbers from 1 to 100, how will you do it? You will have to write document.write 100 times passing values from 1 to 100, which is really time-consuming. You can use JavaScript loops to run the same code a number of times or as long as any condition is true, and each time with a different value. You can also use loops to access items in an array.

There are four different types of loops.

1. for loop
2. for/in loop
3. while loop
4. do....while loop

The 'for' loop is used to repeat a specific set of code until a specific condition becomes false. It is also used commonly to access the elements of an array. The syntax of the 'for' loop is:

```
for(statement1, statement2, statement3)
{
        lines of code to be executed
}
```

Here statement1 is executed before the loop starts, statement2 defines the condition for running the loop, and statement3 is executed each time after the loop is executed. Usually, statement1 is used to assign initial values to variables that are used inside the loop; statement1, statement2 and statement3 are optional.

Example:

```
var x;
for(x=1;x<=50;x++)
{
        document.write(x + "<br />");
}
```

The above lines of code display values from 1 to 50. The following lines of code also execute the same. We omit statement1 and statement3 (semicolon should not be avoided) and managed it outside and inside the 'for' loop.

```
var x = 1;
for(;x<=50;)
{
        document.write(x + "<br />");
        x++;
}
```

You can loop through an array, as given below, to display all the items in the array.

```
<html>
<head>
<title>Loop through Arrays</title>
<script type="text/javascript">
var employees = ["John Smith", "Kevin Young", "Hannah
Rivera", "John Joseph", "Sarah Rose", "Olivia White"]
var i;
for(i=0;i<employees.length;i++)
{
        document.write(employees[i] + "<br />");
}
</script>
</head>
<body>
</body>
</html>
```

The for/in loop is used to loop through the properties of an object. An object is nothing but a collection of key/value pairs. The syntax of the for/in loop is:

```
for(variable_name in object_name
{
        lines of code to be executed
}
```

Here, variable_name is the name of a variable (it can be any name) and the object_name is the name of the object through which you want to loop. Here, variable_name returns all the keys, and object_name[variable_name] returns their corresponding values.

Example:

Suppose you have an object named Employee with the following key/value pairs:

var Employee = {firstName : "John", lastName: "Smith", department: "HR", age: 34, salary: 20000};

You want to write the following lines of code to get the employee details:

```
var employee = {firstName : "John",  lastName:
"Smith", department: "HR", age: 34, salary: 20000};
for(var details in employee)
{
        //details return keys and employee[details]
return corresponding values
        document.write(details + " is <b>" +
employee[details] + "</b>.<br />");
}
```

The 'while' loop is used to execute a set of instructions as long as the specified condition is true. Do not forget to add the code that will make the condition false at some point in time inside the 'while' loop. Otherwise, your loop will never end, and it might even crash your browser. The syntax of the 'while' loop is:

```
while(condition)
{
        lines of code to be executed
}
```

Example:

```
var x = 1;
while(x<=50)
```

```
{
        document.write(x + "<br />");
        x++;
}
```

The 'do...while' loop is similar to the 'while' loop except for the fact that it executes once for sure, even if the condition is false. The syntax of the 'do....while' loop is:

```
do
{
        lines of code to be executed
} while(condition)
```

Example:

```
var x = 1;
do
{
        document.write(x + "<br />");
        x++;
}
while(x<=50)
```

Exercises

1. Display the multiplication table of 6 (6*1, 6*2 up to 6*10).

```
<html>
<head>
<title>Multiplication Table</title>
<script type="text/javascript">

rows = 10;
```

```
var x = 6;
var y = 1;
var output = "<table border='1' width='500'
cellspacing='0'cellpadding='5'>";
// #10005 is the decimal unicode value for cross mark
for(i=1;i<=rows;i++)
{
   document.write(x + " &#10005; " + y + " = " + x*y +
"<br />");
   y++;
}
</script>
</head>
<body>
</body>
</html>
```

If you open the .html file that contains the above lines of code in your browser, you will get an output like this:

```
6  ✕ 1 = 6
6  ✕ 2 = 12
6  ✕ 3 = 18
6  ✕ 4 = 24
6  ✕ 5 = 30
6  ✕ 6 = 36
6  ✕ 7 = 42
6  ✕ 8 = 48
6  ✕ 9 = 54
6  ✕ 10 = 60
```

46

2. Display Fibonacci numbers below 100.

Tip: the Fibonacci series is:

0 1 1 2 3 5 8 13 21 34 55 .... (each number is the sum of the two numbers before it, i.e. 2 = 1 + 1, 3 = 2 + 1, 5 = 3 + 2, etc.)

Solution

```
<!DOCTYPE html>
<html>
<head>
<title>Fibonacci Series</title>
<script type="text/javascript">
var first = 0, second = 1, next;
while(first<100)
{
document.write(first + "<br />");
next = first + second;
first = second;
second = next;
}
</script>
</head>
<body>
</body>
</html>
```

If you open the .html file that contains the above lines of code in your browser, you will get an output like this:

Chapter 8 JavaScript Functions

Many times, you will have to reuse a block of code several times. Functions are the building blocks in any programming language. Functions make your code really reusable and easily manageable. You need to create a function and then call it to get the block of code executed.

To create a function, you need to use the keyword function followed by the name of the function and then parentheses. You then need to write your code enclosed in curly braces. Here is the syntax:

```
function function_name()
{
        lines of code to be executed
}
```

Example:

```
function wishUser()
{
        var today = new Date();
        var hours = today.getHours();

        var wish;
        if(hours<12)
            wish = "Good Morning!!!";
        else if(hours<16)
            wish = "Good Afternoon!!!";
        else
            wish = "Good Evening!!!";
        document.write(wish);
}
```

You will sometimes need some inputs to execute a set of code. You can pass those inputs to your function as parameters. You need to specify the parameters within parentheses after the function name. Here is the syntax:

```
function function_name(para1, para2)
{
        lines of code to be executed
}
```

Example:

```
function findSum(firstNum, secondNum)
{
        var sum = firstNum + secondNum;
        document.write("The sum of " + firstNum + "
and " + secondNum + " is " + sum);
}
```

Most of the time, you need to get the output from the function for further processing instead of printing the output within the function itself using the document.write method. JavaScript allows you to write functions that return some values. You just need to use the keyword return followed by the value to be returned inside the function. Syntax is as below:

```
function function_name(arg1, arg2)
{
        lines of code to be executed
        return actual_value;
}
```

Example:

```
function findSum(firstNum, secondNum)
{
        var sum = firstNum + secondNum;
        return sum;
}
```

Just creating the functions will not do any magic for you. You have to invoke or call the function in order to execute the lines of code in the function. You just need to specify the function name and pass the inputs to the function within parentheses. The actual values you pass to the function are known as arguments. In other words, parameters are the names specified while creating functions, and arguments are the actual values sent to the function.

```
function findSum(firstNum, secondNum)
{
        var sum = firstNum + secondNum;
```

```
        return sum;
}
var num1 = prompt("Enter the first number:");
var num2 = prompt("Enter the second number:");
var result = findSum(parseInt(num1), parseInt(num2));
document.write("The sum of " + num1 + " and " + num2
+ " is " + result);
```

The value received using the prompt box is always a string,
though you enter a number. We need to convert the string value
to an integer using the parseInt method because otherwise, it will
just concatenate the string values and we will not get the
expected result.

Exercise

1. Check whether the value entered by the user is a palindrome or
not. A palindrome is a value that reads the same backwards as
well as forwards. Example: madam

```
<html>
<head>
<title>Palindrome</title>
<script type="text/javascript">
function palindromeCheck(valToCheck)
{
        var reversedVal =
valToCheck.split('').reverse().join('');
        if(valToCheck == reversedVal)
                document.write(valToCheck + " is a
palindrome.");
        else
                document.write(valToCheck + " is not a
palindrome.");
```

```
}
var palCheck = prompt("Enter any value");
palindromeCheck(palCheck);
</script>
</head>
<body>
</body>
</html>
```

Chapter 9 Cookies

What would be the first thing that comes to your mind when you hear the term 'cookie'? It could be a small, sweet biscuit. In programming, a cookie is a small piece of data sent from a website to the Web browser of the person who visits that website. It is later stored in his or her computer. Do you see your email account password or Facebook account password as soon as you enter your user name? If yes, then you are also enjoying the benefits of cookies, though unknowingly.

Why are cookies so relevant and useful? It is mainly because of the stateless nature of the Web. The communication between a Web browser and the Web server (website) happens using a protocol named HTTP – and HTTP is stateless. To make it clear, the user data entered in one Web page will not be available in the next page of a website. Then how are you seeing your name on the top of your Gmail or Yahoo inbox if the Web server cannot maintain it from the login page to your inbox page? Here is where client-side state management enters the picture. There are different techniques for storing state information on your Web browser, and a cookie is one of them.

Cookies are saved as key-value pairs. When data is saved in cookies, the Web browser can get the required details directly from the computer without the hassle of communicating with the Web server each time the data is needed.

It is so easy to create cookies in JavaScript. You can use the document.cookie property. The syntax is:

```
document.cookie = "cookie_name=cookie_value";
```

You can specify an expiry date to the cookie by adding the expires parameter. That way the specific cookie will be removed from the computer on the specified date. The syntax is:

```
document.cookie = "cookie_name=cokkie_value; expires=
     expiry_date";
```

You can also specify the path to which the cookie belongs by adding the path parameter. The syntax is:

```
document.cookie = "cookie_name=cokkie_value; expires=
     expiry_date; path=path;
```

Example:

```
document.cookie = "facebookPassword=mypassword;
expires=Fri, 31 Jan 2015 22:00:00 UTC;path=/"
```

Here a cookie with the key facebookPassword and value mypassword will be stored, which is valid for the entire domain until 31st January 2015 10 PM.

You can access the stored cookie using the document.cookie property itself using the following syntax:

```
var variable_name = document.cookie;
```

If you have 10 cookies stored, then the variable will contain all cookies in this format:

```
cookie1=value; cookie2=value; cookie3=value;
```

You will have to process the variable to get the cookie you need.

You can easily delete a cookie if you do not want it anymore. You just have to set the value of the cookie to empty, and also set the value of expires to a past date.

Exercise

Create a Web page with two textboxes for the user to enter his user name and password, and also an Enter button. When the user enters his user name into the first textbox, if a cookie already exists with the user name entered, then the password should be automatically populated in the password textbox. If there is no cookie, however, save the user name and password into a cookie for 30 days when the user clicks the Enter button.

Tip: Make sure that you run the website from your local server to access it as a website. To do that, keep your file in your inetpub/www folder (if you are using IIS) or xampp/htdocs folder (if you are using Apache), and access the site using localhost/webpage.html.

Solution

```
<html>
<head>
<title>Cookie!!!</title>
<script type="text/javascript">
var alreadyExists = "false";
function createCookie()
{

  var uName =
document.getElementById("txtUser").value;
  // adding site1 to the key name to differentiate it
for this specific website
  var userName = "site1" + uName;
  var pWord =
document.getElementById("txtPassword").value;
  if(document.getElementById("txtUser").value == ""
|| document.getElementById("txtUser").value == null)
        alert("Enter your user name.");
  else
if(document.getElementById("txtPassword").value == ""
|| document.getElementById("txtPassword").value ==
null)
        alert("Enter your password.");
  else
    {
             // if the cookie does not exist
already, create a cookie
             if(alreadyExists == "false")
             {
             saveCookie(userName, pWord);
```

```
                    alert("Your password is saved for
future use!!!");
                    }
                    else
                    {
                        //if the cookie already exists,
just give a welcome back message
                        alert("Welcome back " + uName);
                    }
        }
}
function saveCookie(cookieName, cookieValue)
{
var date = new Date();
/*time after 30 days is current date and time in
milliseconds + 30 days in milliseconds
30 days in milliseconds means 30 days each of 24
hours, 60 minutes, 60 seconds and 1000 milliseconds*/
date.setTime(date.getTime()+(30*24*60*60*1000));
document.cookie = cookieName + "=" + cookieValue + ";
expires=" + date.toGMTString();
}
function checkCookie()
{
if(document.getElementById("txtUser").value == "" ||
document.getElementById("txtUser").value == null)
        alert("Enter your user name.");
else
{
        var userName = "site1" +
document.getElementById("txtUser").value;
        //check whether the specific user name is
saved as a cookie
        var userPass = getCookie(userName);
        if (userPass!="")
        {
```

```javascript
                //if cookie already exists, set the
value of a flag and set the password in the textbox
                alreadyExists = "true";

        document.getElementById("txtPassword").value =
userPass;
        }
}
}
function getCookie(cookieName)
{
var name = cookieName + "=";
//as all cookies are returned separated by semicolon,
splitting the array first
var cookieArray = document.cookie.split(';');
for(var i=0; i<cookieArray.length; i++)
  {
  var check = cookieArray[i].trim();
  //getting the cookie with the required details
  if (check.indexOf(name)==0)
     return
check.substring(name.length,check.length);
  }
return "";
}
</script></head>
<body>
User    Name:    <input    type="text"    id="txtUser"
onblur="checkCookie();"><br />
Password:  <input   type="password"   id="txtPassword"
><br />
<button  id="btnLogin"  onclick="createCookie();">Sign
In</button>
</body>
</html>
```

Copy the above lines of code in a new file and save it as an .html in your local server. Access it using localhost/filename.html. Enter a user name and password and click the button so that it will be saved. Next time, try to enter the same user name and the corresponding password will automatically appear in the password textbox, and when you click the button, you will get a welcome back message.

Chapter 10 The Document Object Model

The Document Object Model (DOM) is a programming interface or standard for accessing HTML and XML documents. The browser creates a DOM of the page when it is loaded, and JavaScript has the power to manipulate this model. You can access and even modify all the elements of an HTML document from JavaScript using HTML DOM. For example, you can get the value entered in a textbox, decide what should happen on the click of a button, add new HTML elements, remove existing elements, or even change the styles of HTML elements just by writing JavaScript code.

HTML DOM offers a number of properties which you can use to get or set values of HTML elements, and also a number of methods that you can use to perform some actions on the HTML elements.

The most commonly used method is `document.getElementById`, and it accesses the HTML element using the id of the element.

You can also access elements using their class name, and the method for that is `document.getElementByClassName` where you need to pass the class name. The `setAttribute` method is useful when you have to set a value of an attribute. Of course, you need to pass the name of the attribute and its corresponding value as the first and second parameters.

You can use the `innerHTML` property to get or set the contents of an element. You can set the value of an element using the `attribute` property. With the help of the `style.property` attribute, you can change the style of an HTML element.

You can also handle different events, such as click, key press, double click, focus, etc., on different elements. The syntax is:

```
document.getElementById(id).onevent=function()
{
lines of code to be executed
}
```

OR

```
document.getElementById(id).addEventListener(event,
function_name)
```

Example:

```
<!DOCTYPE html>
<html>
<head>
<title>DOM Manipulation</title>
<style>
.paras
```

```
{
        color:fuchsia;
        font-size:25px;
}
#first
{
        color:red;
        font-size: 30px;
}
#third
{
        background-color:maroon;
        color:white;
        font-size: 20px;
}
</style>
</head>
<body>
<p id="first">This is my FIRST paragraph!!!</p>
<p class="paras">This is my SECOND paragraph!!!</p>
<p id="third">This is my THIRD paragraph!!!</p>
<p class="paras">This is my LAST paragraph</p>
<button id="btnColor">Change Color</button>
<button id="btnContent">Change Content</button>
<script type="text/javascript">
document.getElementById("btnContent").onclick =
function()
{
        document.getElementById("first").innerHTML =
"The content is CHANGED!!!";
}
document.getElementById("btnColor").addEventListener(
"click", changeColor);
function changeColor()
{
```

```
        var items =
document.getElementsByClassName("paras")
        for(var i=0;i<items.length;i++)
                items[i].style.color = "blue";
}
</script>
</body>
</html>
```

Try clicking the buttons to see the changes in the content and
style of some of the elements.

Exercise

Create a Web page with two textboxes for the user to enter his
first name and last name, and also a Submit button. If the user
tries to enter his last name without entering the first name, then
display an alert message. Similarly, if he tries to click the button
without entering the second name, then also display an alert
message. On the click of the button, if both the names are
entered, then display a welcome message.

Tip: The event that gets triggered when an element gets focus is
focus, and the event that gets triggered when an element loses its
focus is blur. You can check whether the first name is entered on
focus of the second textbox, and whether the last name is entered
on blur of the second textbox.

Solution

```
<!DOCTYPE html>
<html>
<head>
```

```
<title>Event Handling</title>
</head>
<body>
First Name: <input id="txtFirst"><br />
Last Name: <input id="txtSecond"><br />
<button id="btnSubmit"
onclick="displayWelcome();">Submit</button>
<script type="text/javascript">
document.getElementById("txtSecond").onfocus =
function()
{
        if(document.getElementById("txtFirst").value
== "")
                alert("Enter your first name");
}
document.getElementById("txtSecond").addEventListener
("blur", checkLastName);
function checkLastName()
{
        if(document.getElementById("txtSecond").value
== "")
                alert("Enter your last name");
}
function displayWelcome()
{
        var first =
document.getElementById("txtFirst").value;
        var last =
document.getElementById("txtSecond").value;
        if(first != "" & last != "")
                alert("Welcome " + first + " " + last
+ " !!!");
        else if(first == "")
                alert("Enter your first name");
        else if(last == "")
                alert("Enter your last name");
```

```
}
window.onload = function() {
  document.getElementById("txtFirst").focus();
};
</script>
</body>
</html>
```

Chapter 11 Object-Oriented JavaScript

If you analyze real-life requirements, you would understand that most of the time, variables or arrays are not enough to simulate real-life situations. Object orientation can help you create objects that actually simulate real-life objects. Just think of a house. There are many different properties for a house, including the number of rooms, area, floor type, name of the owner, location, and so on. There are also a number of actions, which include calculating tax, calculating painting cost, managing the electricity bill, and so on. JavaScript allows you to create objects that have properties and methods. JavaScript objects keep data as key/value pairs.

It is very easy to create objects in JavaScript, and there are two ways to accomplish this. Given below is the syntax:

```
var object_name = {prop1:val1, prop2:val2, method1:
function(){//lines of code},
method2:function(){//lines of code}};
```

OR

```
var object_name = new Object();
object_name.prop1 = val1;
object_name.prop2 = val2;
object_name.method1  = function()
{
   //lines of code
}
object_name.method2  = function()
{
   //lines of code
}
```

You can easily access the objects by just using the property name. The syntax is:

```
var variable_name = object_name.property_name;
```

Example:

```
<html>
<head>
<title>Objects!!!</title>
<script type="text/javascript">
var house = new Object();
house.owner = "John";
house.noOfRooms = 11;
house.location = "ABC Street, Washington";
house.area = 2034;
house.paintingCost = 1000;
house.paintingCostCalculation = function()
{
//this formula is just to understand the concept
return (house.area * house.paintingCost);
```

```
};

house.displayDetails = function()
{
var cost = house.paintingCostCalculation();
document.write(house.owner + "'s house is located in
" + house.location + ". <br />" +
                              "The total cost for
painting " + house.noOfRooms+ " rooms is " + cost +
".");
};
house.displayDetails();
</script>
</head>
<body>
</body>
</html>
```

Here, as well, we have some restrictions because we need to create different objects for different houses. To clarify, if you want to have the details of another person's (say, Ann's) house, then you should again create a new object, which is really time-consuming. Here is where an object constructor can help you. An object constructor is used to create many objects of one type.

```
<html>
<head>
<title>Object Constructor!!!</title>
<script type="text/javascript">
function House(owner, location, noOfRooms, area,
paintingCost)
{
this.owner = owner;
this.noOfRooms = noOfRooms;
this.location = location;
```

```javascript
this.area = area;
this.paintingCost = paintingCost;
this.paintingCostCalculation = function()
{
//this formula is just to understand the concept
return (this.area * this.paintingCost);
};

this.displayDetails = function()
{
var cost = this.paintingCostCalculation();
document.write(this.owner + "'s house is located in "
+ this.location + ". <br />" +
                              "The total cost for
painting " + this.noOfRooms+ " rooms is " + cost +
".<br /><br />");
}
}
var ho1 = new House("John", "ABC Street, Washington",
11, 2034, 1000);
var ho2 = new House("Ann", "West Street, California",
171, 1540, 800);

ho1.displayDetails();
ho2.displayDetails();
</script>
</head>
<body>
</body>
</html>
```

Here, we accomplished the same task easily and efficiently.

Exercise

Create an Employee object constructor which has four properties (first name, last name, department, and years of experience) and two methods (calculate salary and display details). Calculate the salary based on the department and years of experience (department*years of experience). Create 4 employees with the constructor and display their details.

Solution

```
<html>
<head>
<title>Employee Object Constructor!!!</title>
<script type="text/javascript">
function Employee(firstName, lastName, department,
yearsOfExperience)
{
this.firstName = firstName;
this.lastName = lastName;
this.department= department;
this.yearsOfExperience= yearsOfExperience;
this.calculateSalary = function()
{
var sal1;
if(this.department == "Banking")
        sal1 = 1000;
else if(this.department == "HR")
        sal1 = 800;
else if(this.department == "Accounts")
        sal1 = 900;
return (this.yearsOfExperience * sal1);
};
this.displayDetails = function()
{
```

```
var salary = this.calculateSalary();
document.write("Employee Name: " + this.firstName + "
" + this.lastName + "<br /> Department: " +
this.department
                                    + "<br />Years of
Experience: " + this.yearsOfExperience + "<br
/>Salary: " + salary + "<br /><br />");
};


};
var emp1 = new Employee("John", "Smith", "Banking",
11);
var emp2 = new Employee("Ann", "Turner", "Accounts",
7);
var emp3 = new Employee("Kevin", "Young", "Banking",
8);
var emp4 = new Employee("Sarah", "Rivera", "HR", 6);

emp1.displayDetails();
emp2.displayDetails();
emp3.displayDetails();
emp4.displayDetails();
</script>
</head>
<body>
</body>
</html>
```

If you run the .html page that contains the above lines of code from your browser, you will get a screen like this:

```
Employee Name: John Smith
Department: Banking
Years of Experience: 11
Salary: 11000
```

Employee Name: Ann Turner
Department: Accounts
Years of Experience: 7
Salary: 6300

Employee Name: Kevin Young
Department: Banking
Years of Experience: 8
Salary: 8000

Employee Name: Sarah Rivera
Department: HR
Years of Experience: 6
Salary: 4800

Other Books by the Author

SQL for Beginners

http://www.linuxtrainingacademy.com/sql-book

Knowing how to craft SQL queries and navigate your way around a database is an essential skill if are a database administrator, system administrator, or programmer.

SQL for Beginners guides you step-by-step by teaching you how to create databases, populate those databases with data, extract just the data you need, and much more. The book uses plain, clear, and concise language all geared to helped you learn SQL in the easiest manner possible.

Additional Resources

Common Coding Problems Solved Using JavaScript
http://www.linuxtrainingacademy.com/javascript-guide/

As a thank you for reading this book, I would like to give you a free copy of "Common Coding Problems Solved Using JavaScript." It's a perfect complement to this book and will help you along your JavaScript journey.

Create Your Own Programming Language
http://linuxtrainingacademy.com/create-your-own-language

A System To Achieve Every Programmer's Dream. Learn How To Create A Simple Programming Language In A Few Days With This Easy Step-by-step Guide

Learn Programming: from Novice to JavaScript Guru in 2 Weeks
http://www.linuxtrainingacademy.com/javascript-guru

This video training course is a step-by-step guide with all the tools and resources you need to master all your web projects with ease and confidence.

Learning JavaScript Programming Tutorial: A Definitive Guide
http://www.linuxtrainingacademy.com/javascript-definitive

In this training course you will learn the basics of programming with JavaScript, the worlds most used programming language. The tutorial is designed for the absolute beginner - no prior JavaScript programming experience is required in order to get the most out of this video training.

The Ultimate Guide To Node.js + Express
http://www.linuxtrainingacademy.com/nodejs-express

Learn all you need to know about programming with Node and Express so you can build a JavaScript web app quickly.

Appendix

Appendix A: Trademarks

JavaScript is a trademark of Oracle Corporation.

Linux® is the registered trademark of Linus Torvalds in the U.S. and other countries.

Mac and OS X are trademarks of Apple Inc., registered in the U.S. and other countries.

UNIX is a registered trademark of The Open Group.

Windows is a registered trademark of Microsoft Corporation in the United States and other countries.

All other product names mentioned herein are the trademarks of their respective owners.

www.ingramcontent.com/pod-product-compliance
Lightning Source LLC
Chambersburg PA
CBHW071028050326
40689CB00014B/3573